VAULT

a poem

VAULT

a poem

❀

KATHLEEN
PEIRCE

NEW MICHIGAN PRESS
TUCSON, ARIZONA

NEW MICHIGAN PRESS

DEPT OF ENGLISH, P. O. BOX 210067

UNIVERSITY OF ARIZONA

TUCSON, AZ 85721-0067

<http://newmichiganpress.com>

Orders and queries to <nmp@thediagram.com>.

Copyright © 2017 by Kathleen Peirce.
All rights reserved.

ISBN 978-1-934832-60-8. FIRST PRINTING.

Printed in the United States of America.

Design by Ander Monson.

Cover image: "Statuette of Daphne" (Design: Wenzel
Jamnitzer, Execution: Abraham Jamnitzer, Nuremberg,
between 1579 and 1586). Photo by Jürgen Karpinski /
bpk Bildagentur / Grünes Gewölbe, Staatliche Kunstsam-
mlungen Dresden / Art Resource, NY.

CONTENTS

Vault   1

Notes by section   53
Acknowledgments   57

I.

In a dry time, one night's rain was felt to fall to her
who lay awake in bed, inside no darker air than what
the rain fell through entirely, hers because one waits,
one pays with waiting, as outside, late in winter,
it may be the long-dried uncut grass is touched by
an almost evenhanded, reasonable water
each leaf has given something to by bending
so, by bending down. Say her body moved that way,
night and the one dark lowering again,
and inside her mind the blades fell through
while outside in blades of water,
on leaves one knows as blades, rain fell
as if in thought, in air.

2.

Abraham Jamnitzer is long dead,
and his father before him, and his father,
and his father, and— Here stands
a silver statuette with arms raised up.
At her silver bodice, waist, and hem,
silver medallions wearing silver faces shine
from this figure so admired
at a father's hand, a son made her again,
a duplicate, almost. Her hands appear
just come undone, remade as coral-made,
in red. No cameo; this is consubstantiation;
hands as branches from another element
where coral moves, or moved, would move,
handbranches/branchhands;
her coral looks arterial, and from her head, a spray
of coral lives again because arranged
as could be spokes of spoken sentences made visible,
except her mouth's made closed. They might be thoughts
whose ends are new. One wants to sleep.

3.

One wants to sleep, though sleep reveals another spray
ingrown, regrown every night, seeming to move
in the non-air of dream's most perfect privacy
where any thought can marry any form, so
even while falling there, if the paw one loves the odor of
more than wet grass itself, if a paw is raised
and scraped against the door,
someone wants out, someone wants in,
never some*thing.* A paw is raised again,
comes down in dream as the memory of a book close to the ear
falling from the hand whose wrist she mouthed,
of who loved her, dead now eleven years,
or it may be a branch pushed to the roof by wind. Rain comes
to roofs as though ceilings are doors. Should she feel, waking, that
she loved, or loves? The moment the coral branch was
fixed in the cuff, a wrist was what?
A roughening of the silver has inferred
some lacework there.

4.

On an isthmus of a kind,
one abbey in far Austria, buttercream and yellow
(*no, buttercream and apricot, Abess,*
it was Sanssouci that was so over-yellow),
contains, as no other place, the footfalls
of Maria Theresa. It was Sanssouci
that was so over-yellow. Without
a care. This abbey's corridor goes on, goes on,
the arches made to hold as they appear to narrow
while never narrowing, not unlike the way a figurine
contains the figure of a girl, arms high, breasts high—
Must she always wear shoes? She must. Think them,
behind her silver hem, unlaced, tangled, at root.

5.

Heel-clicks, Baroque.
Empress Maria Theresa comes in presentation of her gift.
Behold :: unveiled, dead,
two of the eternally devout: a pair long buried, unearthed,
undressed,

6.

redressed in lace and silk. *Laces and silks.* Posed so,
sidelong, apart, in glass tombs, sealed,
sacrosanct, they face across the abbey church
at the station those assembling feel
as half-way down the aisle. *Pass through.*

7.

Pass through. Look left and feel the other waiting from the right,
look right and feel the other way around. Laces
and silks. He bears a quill-tip pen. *Are there jewels?* There are.
At her neckline, cuff, and finger bone, a red-brown
garnet radiance—*Why is the unearthed beautiful?*
lit garnets encircled with a perfection of seed pearls—
That were his eyes? No,
his eyes are nothing in his skull. *And yet they look?*
They seem to look. They seem as the poet sees
birds occur because the air dissolves itself
as birds. Or is it air congealed? So dense,
reality, a thing can form by what breaks there
as well as if it binds.
That were his eyes? Yes.
Yes and sweeten it. His eyes rest at her wrist,
her throat, her hand, in perpetuity. *So
and not so. Her true body is not there. Nor his.*
Nor his.

8.

[…She inherited from her grandmother the dark complexion
and the piercing black eyes of the March family. She was of
peculiar characteristics, herself attributing some of them to
the supposed Indian blood in the Marches. She was a devoted
lover of nature, with which she spent many pleasant hours in
sweet communion, in the fields and forests near her pleasant
home. At the time of her tragic death she lived alone in her
pretty cottage in the fork of the roads leading from Pepperell
to East Pepperell. In the early evening of the 6th of January,
1883, the house took fire from some unknown cause, and before
aid could be rendered it was consumed. Miss Chase perished
in the flames which destroyed many valuable relics of by-gone
days…]

9.

If *brightness is a truce*, a sleepless woman
is a flowing audience, and a made thing.
In a sentence about the river, she says,
"A mirror brought outdoors is also a light-chime."
In a sentence about who would be looking in, she writes,
"A flake of salmon, salmon-colored, lifted to the actual mouth
of one who'd kissed her in a dream."

10.

She remembers when there was no water. The rocks were whiter.
She could still see the day lily, still think of the morning glory
as gesturing in other things. Tallied from her first planting, when
mistaken, all, for weeds, and pulled, the heap of ruined tendrils
magnified her looking at the finally first-come, cone-shaped buds;
their spiral narrowing added, the thinnest leaf,
the star retained at the wholly opened rim, all added, profusion
added by midday, the singing, sobbing blue added, and
each like each with one gesture for infinity, the throats so white,
the scent negligible, added, the clinging, added, the daily ending,
added, the blue exhaling into fuchsia, the late flesh blown,
the inexplicable rewind of the thing, backward and looser
but the same motion in return, added, until she heard
she had been wheeled under an arch of these each summer day
at eight months old. Her mother spoke the words,
who speaks no more. No sum.
It may be the long-dried uncut grass is touched by
an almost evenhanded, reasonable water
each leaf has given something to by bending
so, by bending down.

11.

Abraham Jamnitzer is long dead, may be a pearl,
two pearls, a leaf of grass, a laurel tree. Coral was thought
essential, quintessential, nature's perfect child,
touching *(touched by)* all three realms.
Her limbs: the right leg is exposed. Her silver thigh
shines out from underneath her silver gown. The other seems
to live inside. Her silver sleeves, at elbow length, are puffed,
and banded twice. One red hand/branch is split
three ways; one four, with two emerging nubs.
Pliny, *Natural History*, Book II: *not even for God*
are all things possible—for he cannot, even if he wishes,
commit suicide… The power of nature is what we mean

12.

by the word God.…hail is produced from frozen rain
and snow from the same fluid less solidly condensed,
but hoar frost from cold dew; snow falls during winter
but not hail, and hail itself falls more often in the daytime
than at night, and melts much faster than snow;
mists do not occur in summer, nor in extremely cold weather,
nor dew in frosty or very windy weather, and only on fine nights;
liquid is reduced in bulk by freezing, and when ice is thawed
the bulk is not the same; variations of colour and shape
are seen in clouds in proportion as the fire mingled with them
gains the upper hand.

13.

Again, a veiled baby,
one of many, one December,
will see the end of a century
with a pinched face
under a drapery of flames,
hair held in the hands again
as the hungry open their bags
of roses regarding air
a thousand thousand times, even
before birth, but also after
death, which rains
on our village, where we live.

14.

Enter peach-like wearing yellow, buttercream,
coral, apricot, and salmon, you bridesmaids of speech;
her eyes have yet to be described. Gestured in
other things, the sobbing blue? Look up. No sum. It is
to suffer here. Who looks where the dying look
look at the world, but without the air
of the unworldly as it swells. Who looks
at a body held by death and finds words more faithful
than that groom and bride? No one. No words,
no hand to give or take away, no upper hand.

15.

Without a care. White petal
on white petal, in porcelain,
one flower on a coiled stem
holds one candle, never lit, a
white flower with an effect
of after-white, given to
grey-white in the folds, and
redoubled in the mirror as a mantelpiece.
Look up. Repeated flower stems unwind
ad infinitum as a chandelier.
It blurs one's sense
of singularity. It is an affluence,
an edifice, a sense, not an idea,
of transformation's start.
Look back. Remember? *No, look back*
to your solitary mantelpiece.

16.

One sees the mirror, finally, rather than the self
reflected back, or that first pale flowering, and sees
the mirror also framed in porcelain
buttercups and primroses, but
with their color drained—
and that the walls bear plaster-frosted
creepers and leaves and flower heads,
white-on-white-on-white-on-white
in bas-relief. *Relief*—

17.

I received him in the dark. I had come to bear everything
bar being seen. Behold :: a naked, finger-long, ivory boy
seated on an ivory skull would make, if he could breathe,
a perfect ivory bubble with his pipe.
He doesn't wear but *is* the crown of "Contrefait Sphere
with an Allegory of Transience," Jacob Zeller,
Dresden, 1611. Here, bone is flesh, off-white as if off-white
was pushed from white by force into a further force
barely restrained in his raised legs, raised arms,
blown hair. The skull he sits on brings bone back to bone again,
but under it revolves, or would revolve, if we could touch,
a virtuoso piece. A turner shapes and hollows out
a bone-sphere by machine. From scrap he carves portrait
    medallions
to see behind round windows in the sphere. In Zeller's
    "Contrefait,"
the portraits live *inside* inside, in an incised, revolving *if we*
    could touch it
world inside a world inside a world. One is not free to turn
and not turn in, turn into, turn away, turn back. The prince

18.

is dead at twenty-seven, green-white as a linden bloom.
A sister whimpers though she drowned.
A daughter wakes to feel her mouth foam-filled
as her mother dies in a distant bed.
Drought in summer. Lightning without rain, and then
a rain, and then long rain.

19.

Still stands our silver girl.
Her stillness stills the moving world in waves,
a blind eye rolling on a crowd
of sighted faces, felt to be
a kind of sight to those it does not see;
a bell hammered
in copper, dangling a wooden tongue:
it never rings;
one thinks one knows the sound.
Her arms are up. When rain falls, it falls
without once touching her. Her coral hands and thoughts appear
diffused because a coral widened undersea.

20.

Under all rocks,
something—see
even under water under a
river rock a wet-
ness but see what
is thought of one
who would look
for wetness there, or
for dryness in drought time.
To some end what
water did or what dry air was was
less unloved, more
unthought of, not so un-
seen as effortlessly known
and so thought turned away. No
language needed there.

21.

[On the 19th of May, 1780, memorable in New England as
The Great Dark Day, about 10 o'clock, A.M., the sky became
exceedingly dark, the air apeared heavy and thick, so much
so that in passing the hand from right to left there was a
pressure never before known to exist.]

22.

Rain-sick now. The driest summer still
in mind. Wettest summer heaves and pours
so. Under water, under a
river rock, wetness loves a blur,
and there the water waters
what, itself? And in this denseness, purity?
The lovely gaze where every eye doth dwell.
Under her rigid silver bodice, no thought has
pulled her nipple hard. No heel-click
as she comes in presentation of…
Enough! Too much, a saturation, and still
the mind makes wide for the sound beyond
the sense of hearing, sight the closed eye
finds form for. The mind vaults there. *And yet?*
And yet one goes so long untouched. *And yet
in all the longing years, something,
something was always palpable
and touching you.*

23.

Something should mark the entrance.
One goes through. An arch, a portico,
a bloody amnion, dark-wet shifting to light-dry,
a monument, a hardening, a hinge,
no less the flat hand put between the shoulder blades
than the feeling of it gone, the feel
of being watched while one looks, museum-feeling,
and sexual, then the feeling gone,
the private feel of looking as the ground is opened up,
a look that would be a light, an auger of bare sight
bearing everything, able to.

[and entered the darkness alone, without a companion.

By the time he reached the end of the first league

the darkness was total, nothing behind or before]

24.

[He made his way, companionless, to the end

of the second league. Utterly lightless, black.
There was nothing behind or before, nothing at all.

Only the blackness pressed in upon his body.
He felt his blind way through the mountain tunnel,]

[I geue to my son Joshua morse all my carte wheles
dung pot plow harrow
youkes chains houes forkes shovel spad grin stone yt as
allso on father bed]

25.

[struggling for breath, through the third league, alone,
and companionless through the fourth, making his way,

and struggling for every breath, to the end of the fifth,
in the absolute dark, nothing behind or before,]

[which he lieth on with a boulster and pillo and a pair
of blinkets and courlitt
and tou pair of shetes a bed sted and mat a pot and a
brass cetell the best of tou
cettels and a belmetel scillet and tou platars and a
paringer and a drinking pot]

26.

[the weight of the blackness pressing in upon him.
Weeping and fearful he journeyed a sixth league,

and, blind, to the end of the seventh league, alone,
without a companion, seeing nothing at all,]

[and tou spoons and the water pails and barils and tobes
all these about
named I geve to my son Joshua and his eires of his own
body begotten]

27.

[weeping and fearful, struggling to keep breathing.
At the end of the eighth league he cried aloud]

[and his eaires of his own body begoten lawfully.]

28.

[of his bones are coral made]

29.

It was like being approached by something fragile
from a long way off. Not the first match
that failed on the candle, the second
that brought it alive with a touch. Less
the rooster known from over the valley,
more the gap in the dawn after one's own dies,
the third breeze that has to bend the fire
down the wick, the value of a thought
of iridescence skimming the breast
and the head held back, a feather of hair
in one hand, scissors in another, not the heart
beating, but what might return over the heart.

30.

[…a stone, often a crystal shape, possessing a light tinge
rather like the color of water in a swimming pool;
a stone with a dark green skin;
a yellowish green stone
characterized by a degree of lubricity.
After being cut and polished,
diamonds of the first and second types
usually lose their greenish color
to become white gems, or
light yellow stones known as "silvery capes."]

31.

First Fall night. *Mark it, nuncle.*
First owl heard again from the same high place,
high dark, and close. *So mark'd.*

32.

One across. Four letter word
for the soft gem that carries fire and water:
opal.
Three down. Five letters, Spanish for ink:
tinta.
Two cats, one black:
Opal, Tinta.

33.

In one room only
one can sit with one's back to
the bed where his sweet hand again
began to enter her and he drowsed,
and slept, and she, held so, kept still. One can
be brought to feel what happened there.
One across. Opal and Tinta pass the same
among the thresholds of the rooms.
One, then the other one.

34

In the barrios, a slur:
too far dark-skinned, ugly:
tinto, tinta.

[The curtains were burning. And the windows had
shattered… My father asked me what I wanted to save
from the flat and I said my dolls' pram and my school bag.
These were saved.]

35.

day

   two yellow butterflies

lit on each   other
two   as two
tumbled up   fast out
of view

36.

Behold :: two bright glass bubbles, pierced by an upright golden stem.
"Sphere with the Singer Orpheus and Little Clockwork"
Glass, gold, enamel, brilliant cut diamonds, rubies, rock crystal.
Georg Benhart
Augsburg, 1575

The bottom sphere encloses Orpheus with a halved and rejoined
rind of glass, its hinges worked
in gold, with long pins wearing top-curls to invite
unpinning, though the world outside the sphere
is effortlessly touchable…
On top the downward-cupped, enamelled base, in fixed parade
encircling the central stem, one finds an eye-sized, enamelled,
    golden stag,
a monkey holding jewels, and a dog.
The fourth animal is missing. All look up
to Orpheus' sphere of self-plus-animals, so clean
inside what has been made to close around.
He strains, looks up as do the captive animals, his animals,
and the golden tree, his tree, is felt to strain. His open legs
suggest his gait. His lyre, held so. We think we know the sound.

37.

We are beside the sound we think we'd know to hear.
On top, a smaller sphere contains the clock, the time
that Orpheus makes true by his attention from below,
while from above it, Saturn's lance-tip falls.
Has fallen. It rests to touch
the clockwork sphere just where it bears a black enamelled belt of
roman numerals from one to twelve. *What turns to tell?* The god. His
body does, and is the key for winding-up.

38.

Lucretius, *De Recum Natura*, Book V:
But since there has to be, at last, an end
Of parturition, earth has given up
Like a worn-out old woman; time does change
The nature of the whole wide world. One state
Develops from another; not one thing
Is like itself forever; all things move…

39.

one, then the other one

40.

[Although the Dresden Orpheus Clock appears to be
unique, it is nearly an identical replica of another
made entirely of rock crystal, the duke's Saint Nicholas gift
to his wife Anna, 1573.]

41.

Her eyes have yet to be described.
Silver-wrought, yes. Behind them, coral is thought hardening.
And the eyelids? Silvery capes. *Saying so is theft. Silvery capes
are diamonds, like the Dresden Green.* Her eyelids are
silver-wrought, and heavy sad. *And her brow?*
Silver-wrought, and deep. *Why look?* To love
the world. *No, why does she look?* To love the world.

42.

[*People were running … between them you could
hear the fearful screaming of the beasts that had been tied to
fences and trees after being freed from their stables. Nevertheless, we
thought the worst was over. Against my instructions, Trude Sarrasani
had her valuable Lipizzaner horses and other animals taken down to
the banks of the Elbe. She herself rushed off to her apartment, to sal-
vage her personal effects. Then the second attack came: more unex-
pected, more intense and more terrible than the first. In the short time
available, it was not possible to put all the animals back in their stalls,
and we could give no thought to the ones down by the river. Everyone
rushed headlong into the air raid shelter.*]

[*Attempts to extinguish the blaze were hopeless. We could only save
what we could. The beasts that we had been able to return to their
stalls before the second raid had remained uninjured, but now they
had to be rescued from the rapidly spreading fire. This was only
partly possible. The tigers, in their travelling cages, died pitifully in
the flames; we had to abandon our attempts to save them…*]

43.

[*On the morning of 14 February, we collected the dead from the Elbe meadows and laid them out on the elephant podium. Since at this point the entire circus building was open to all, strangers—people from the neighborhood—brought their own dead and likewise laid them out on the podium…*]

[*In the middle of the square was the round circus building… The building was burning fiercely and was collapsing even as we watched. In a nearby street I saw a terrified group of dappled circus horses with brightly coloured trappings standing in a circle close to each other.*]

44.

night, and the one dark lowering again

45.

one thinks one knows the sound

46.

And if we ever felt stood on the prospect
of a great love, all that had not happened yet in love
pressed from behind as prior disappointment,
and we understood each moment happened
just the one time, upon it,
the one way, and was possibly remembered wrong,
while from before us pressed all things in moments taking form
by accident, yet recognizable between two kinds,
or with intent but finally not ours,
or with intent and recognizable as ours
but unable to be shared, and some no less astonishing
than tigers or fire, some a lesser fire,
or nothing, almost, as in a stone that carries the most water
merely a stone, good for nothing but to turn in the light.

47.

someone wants out, someone wants in

48.

Yellow
yellow-orange
orange-yellow
orange
yolk, a round inside an oval, crack it out,
and from below the breasts
up to the collar and across,
to measure, yoke,
and to bear
as on animal shoulders, yoke,
for oneself or for another, or for the others,
passed onto, to carry, worn
not as a wing is. Feather-far.

49.

If the quill-end can be said to be a feather's tip
as likely as the end-point of the vane, let it also be
interior, at the rachis-end that stops inside the vane;
let the eye rest there
on the plumulaceous portion; let play the iridescences
that ripple barbs onto barbules in matrixes of slenderness
as of a deer's neck shook like foil with each swallow
of torn flowers down the throat.
Then to the after-feathers, wilder
after the main.

50.

Ever felt a feather wet?

51.

Her eyes have yet to be described.

52.

May 4, 1705, Leipzig Fair. Prince Augustus purchases
a gilded egg with clasp and hinge
in which he finds a golden hen
with clasp and hinge,
and in the hen
a crown.

53.

[(the sawmarks of those teeth
on the stunned heart)]

54.

[(Oh, the sawing of those teeth
against the stunned, numb heart!)]

55.

To meet the unmet lover
prepare two blindfolds, cut and sewn by hand.
Brown, his; hers red,
with shapes embroidered where the lashes brush;
add highly-colored pom-poms, circles circling the hem
to decorate the brink of having everything, and to tap
the forehead and the cheek. To dangle there. Death
is with us everywhere, and was, and was the theme also
of Durer's "Wing of a Blue Roller," though one sees green
making up most of its underside, which is exposed,
green going delicately yellow, framed in black
or blackish-blue, but the route of severing is red. Sweet Christ,
is everything removed? *Everything is broken.*
Reddish feathers growing at the joint, the pronged hand
remind, supply.

56.

swee swee swee the art, swee
the art, sweetheart

57.

what are you doing there
branch by branch
some sky never or always touching you
some ground

58.

Behold :: "Display Bowl with Children's Bacchanal"
Agate, gold, enamel, pearls, diamonds.
Johan and Georg Dinglinger, two brothers.
Dresden, 1711

Everything is broken. Inside this dish, the one white beech, in miniature,
enamelled, stands for woods, and is sawed through above the children's
heads, and peeled below the cut. Count the age rings if you like.
Three boys are in the woods with pants pulled down.
Their torsos are distended baroque pearls, one each,
nacre-slick and white as though pearl-white was drawn from
water almost grey, near green, but pearls are pulled from flesh.
Where is it wrong to look? The middle boy has let himself fall forward
from behind a goat whose golden horns
outmeasure their spread legs. Two images divided lead to three;
above their art a single swan is opening its beak. At left,
another boy has fallen, backwards-down. His pearl's exposed,
his drum has rolled away. His face? All mouth, all (could we hear it) cry,
his teeth are gold, and his brown dog rears up to have at him.
Far right, the third boy has arrived, seems made of entering; his open legs
suggest his gait. His left hand grips a staff, his right a mask, a face
too far beyond his distant manliness. Before his face
he holds *an ancient, glittering face.*

59.

Behold :: "Bowl with Leaf-Shaped Handles," 1715, removed
from allegory, faces, from wit and threat and perfidy.
It marks the failed mill Augustus, king by now, entrusts
his alchemist and engineer to oversee, grinding and polishing
the precious stones of Saxony. *It* is of chalcedony,
one piece, honey-hued, but honey poured on dirt.
It opens wide and low. Its thinness is unbearable,
makes the eye curl round the rim again, relieved again
catching the nick there. Unbearable thinness in the body
of the bowl, made shallow because thinness is depth enough
if one can be unveiled to a veil. Unlayering mind,
and entering hand, and the one stone
turning on the wheel. Gotten so thin,
why not go more, incise in a pattern there,
a perfect chain of entrances that will not pass fully through,
a thought extended to stone handle-leaves that wing out from the sides,
two as two, identical and opposite, held still in undulation
to meet the fingers of who bears to lift this thing
to light, which passes through. *Pass through.*

60.

The childhood toy, and tree, and pew,
the heap of snow so moved to memory
by a few green once-low stems
of lily-of-the-valley, bent so under a weight
of tiny bells of frag-
rance, heavy or not, but put,
not like morels (to mouth), to nose, there
in the small bud vase before the Virgin Mary
on the Singer never used by three at once,
but sometimes two, when learning, and
none of it blue, though the snow at night had
seemed so, and the lily bells in TV light,
and the Virgin, inescapably, even painted all
bride-white, and the missing sister, dead at birth,
and the one born after her, always, but more as her own
weather than a color one could see and tell
or not; the child was blue.

61.

The sister whimpers though she drowned.
The titmouse flies each sunflower seed
to one cut branch to crack it and eat it
so as to return? One feast is more delicious
than another, the next one always best;
one featherheaded shape the more adorable
among the birds. But one titmouse among
the titmice blurs, one whimpering is heard
as sussuration, without words. Words miss; just
say the sunflower hangs its head and watch
what ignores you.
Two sisters come into the family room
to sing, to practice it. Pose, struck. Chord,
struck. And how the youngest misses.
Now, a three part harmony, with two parts audible.
Now, a round. *Come in after the fourth note*
as when, between two turning playground ropes
you stepped, and were inhabited, disclosed.
Rose, Rose, Rose, Rose

62.

rose, rose, rose, rose

63.

her arms are up

64.

each leaf has giv-

65.

en something to

66.

the five-pronged hand

67.

Sister, the fawns come
less afraid on gray days than on bright
to eat, to eat
the springtime buds. Delicious flower
after delicious flower. One dawn,
one daughter took what were a mother's arms, and washed,
after the mother's afterlife was born into the room. Four roses. Five.
One took the face.

68.

Behold :: an ivory statuette.
"Mercury and Putto"
Adam Lanckhardt
Vienna, mid 17th century

Far from his animal, we see that he was made from it.
So things come close to other things. Form collects, reflects,
and cannot still. A left foot has come forward like stopped thought.
The putto kneels to strap the winged shoe. Everything
is added to. This cherub weighs a boy, a man, a bird, an elephant.
His baby-gaze is heavenward, but just above his head, the scrotum of a god
seems to insist. This messenger is young: poured cream,
hard milk, soft bone, browned only at the ankle-wings
and helmet-wings, all that which makes his body garnitured.
The caduceus is gray and intertwined by snakes so looped
as to present one creature with two heads.
His helmet bears a face he cannot wear.
There are too many possibilities for pure idea here,
though this god's freer arm is at its limit, reaching up.
Up, the pointer finger points. All wings are adamant. Could fly. Will.
All form collects. All flight is genital.

69.

Pliny, *Natural History*, Book IX: ...*they show so many differences of colour, and also of shape—being flat, hollow, long, crescent-shaped, circular, semi-circular, humped, smooth, wrinkled, serrated, furrowed; with the crest bent into the shape of a purple, the edge projecting into a sharp point, or spread outwards, or folded inwards; and again picked out with stripes or with flowing locks or with curls, or parted in little channels or like the teeth of a comb, or corrugated like tiles, or reticulated into lattice-work, or spread out slantwise or straight, close-packed, diffused, curled; tied up in a short knot, or linked up all down the side, or opened so as to shut with a snap, or curved so as to make a trumpet.*

70.

Behold :: "Cherry Pit Carved with One Hundred Eighty-Five Heads"
Anonymous, 1595

A mirabilia! We have a wonderwork in gold, enamel,
pearl, and cherry pit, where, so small, and
cheek-to-cheek, these faces can be said
to have held on to their bones,
the sort that thinking puts inside a mirror and recoils from,
How many faces are there in a face?
and these faces can be seen as pressed by other faces all the way
(not far) around, all of which, of whom, (if they could see) they
could not see,
not face. Some press sidelong
against a faceless skull. All
in all, it bears a mounting
as if to have been made
an earring of.

71.

[He will not tell of the difficulties of his labor.
More than once he cried out to the vault above
that it was impossible … A god, he reflected,
must speak but a single word, and in that word
there must be "absolute plenitude."]

72.

[(According to a recent count of heads,
there are only one hundred thirteen.)]

73.

We were lost, and looking for the one we said was lost.
We held ourselves against the body of a stream
as though its surface wanted us.
We floated there. We floated belly-down. We floated down.
Our teacher told us to. We were astute regarding surfaces,
but looking forward, out.
Banks held the stream. Trees held the banks.
The roots of cypresses exposed themselves
as half-dry giant locks of hair. Why locks?
Who hasn't seen a locket holding hair,
or seen a face inside, in miniature, and felt enormous
things? In time there was a shape ahead,
a torso, waist-high in the water, bending over it
the way a dancer would, a movement ending in a pose
for looking at. And then we saw it was a tree. And then
a flock of house wrens settled in,

74.

the sweetness of their faces round and red, but gently red,
unlike the cardinals, and absolutely sad.
Behind us, splashing started up, splashing and laughter,
laughing and splashter, and we knew the lost one
had found us, and was a stranger to our mood.
It was as though a blade was drawn across the stream,
dividing mood from mood, an incontestable blade of glass,
but dragged across the surface as a wing.

75.

Behold :: "The Throne of the Grand Mogul Aureng-Zeb"
Wood core, gold, silver, gilt, steel, enamel, precious stones,
rock crystal, pearls, lacquer.
Johann Melchior Dinglinger and workshop
Georg Friedrich Dinglinger
Dresden, 1701-1708

Stand back. *Come close.*
Ten square feet. Three courts. 4,909 diamonds,
160 rubies, 164 emeralds, one sapphire, sixteen pearls,
and two cameos. It is as enormous a miniature
as any life, but it resists verisimilitude
with perfect symmetry. There is a populace. Everyone from A to Z
is helpless in desiring an audience with Aureng-Zeb. There is ever
a populace; each desire, being desire, bears a gift.
A whole morning flies into each mouth with each colossal breath.
As if in thought, in air.

76.

If the Lord arrives by way of wings,
the corresponding gift begins in taking flight
and being caught. Or try and seem made stilled; try to
make radiance while fearing not. *A mirror*
brought outdoors is also a light-chime;

77.

two mirrors mark the entrance of *Grand Court.*
They face across the widest place, the starting place,
but angle in resistance of a locked infinity,
the only oppulence that could outsparkle this, this
static shimmering crowd of men with men, men with elephants,
gold men in matching, silver, noble, ceremony hats,
silver men in golden a-line robes, men so close to majesty
they would feel part of it; one feels majestic looking down at men,
men with parasols held against the glare, with turbans, corbels, casks,
amulets, embroideries, carved buttons, confits, goblets, relishes,
bracelets made of hair with fasteners of ivory or tortoise shell,
with tortoises, watchworks, ostrich feather fans, tapestries and figurines,
sweetmeats, best shoes, swords-in-sheath, two cameos,
two palanquins, each carrying one girl. One sapphire,
water-blue. *A sleepless woman is a flowing audience,*
and a made thing. So figures in a place become the place.

78.

A kiss begins with a first
droplet, Lord, of silence.

79.

The first of these is the mouth of.
Close to the island of that name,
at which the nearest channel, called
the Holy River, is swallowed up
in a marsh nineteen miles in extent.
The second is called Fair Mouth.
The third, next to the island of.
The fourth, False Mouth.
Then comes the island of.
Afterwards, the North Mouth
and the Barren Mouth. These mouths
are each of these so large
that for a distance of forty miles
the sea is overpowered
and the water tastes fresh.

80.

One sees the mirror, finally, rather than the self
reflected back.
As one resolves the sight of branches
coming out the head of deer?
Yes, and sweeten it.
Resemblance is intended. Silver-grey, bark-brown, branched-out,
animal motion makes animals seem themselves
and not themselves as branches any longer. One sees
the fur. The antlers, mirrors of each other.

Still stands our silver girl.

81.

Snow. High dark, and cold.
Mark it, nuncle.
Dark makes the flakes fall whiter. *Yes.*
Inertial frame makes the falling feel like this
is happening to us. *Yes.* There are so many. There is
heartsease, ataraxis, in never being able to see them all,
or any one for long. *Yes.*
One light, near full, high-hung. *Yes.*
Touching us. *Yes.*
Head-in-the-clouds or no. *Yes.*
And there is a street lamp. *Yes.* Widened gyre of light.
So mark'd.

82.

We saw snow flakes as light flakes, chipped off and sifted onto us,
a cold inside a calmer cold our bodies' heat made disappear. So many
more than many fell. We saw the trees, the street, a wicker chaise
made fresh. We said the flakes fell lightly,
but we said the snow fell hard. Accrual, accrual,
attar of the baroque! Axis of identity! The chaise,
long made a shape able to be put upon, now showed,
under the streetlamp's cone of light and snow,
each highlit strand of willow as so fine, made bent against,
into, around itself. We said snow cushioned something there, and saw
someone with a fan of roses step out from the dark,
lay roses where a torso might have found repose. Shoulders, a yoke, a head,
crown of a head, a face, a mind, a sight, a thought. Red roses, snow.

83.

In the gap our thinking made, another flower carrier approached.
Madonna of blue flowers, watch us as we look! A blaze of daffodils
was carried baby-like in arms and laid against the red. Next came
the nodding tulip heads, white on white on white, and a tall one put
sunflowers, heavy there. There were upended ballgown skirts of peonies
with center-tongues from pink to purple-red,
and one undid a bunch of violets from a coat
and laid them down. More came. Thick wildflower bouquets, too much
for one hand, fine nets of queen anne's lace, wild carrot, cattail,
foxglove, rue, were softly, singly lowered down. Alium and zinnia,
lowered down. And the fragile were spoken for and carried in:
poppies in flames, rain lilies, anemones, hibiscus, primroses,
then the sturdier lavender was laid by, beside that green one, asphodel.
Gladiolus, blooming in succession from the inmost out, were piled on
where dandelion lay beside gardenia, freesia, buttercup.
Stargazers, tigers burned. The tiny hanging bells of frag-
rant lily-of-the-valley dangled there. More came, with apple-scented
chamomile, with clovers, thistles, baby's breath, ranunculus. Chrysanthemum
was heaped by bachelor button, bittersweet, forget-me-not, and every shade of
color-heavy rose, all brought by passing flower carriers to a wicker chaise
in snow that bore up flowers on flowers on flowers until not one more could

84.

hold, until we were remade as them. Behold ::

85.

An image of gentians could be thought
a violence to violets whose shadow-lives
lie further back, in gatherings of themselves
among all greens not theirs, in grassy childhoods
and afterlives of places, where
tender buds on tender stems now bring
two hands-full of tender thoughts about them,
thoughts that, by middle age, might be excused
to the privacy of memory where thinking back
resembles looking down. Two hands, and far
more flowers unpicked than thoughts of them. It may be
the whitest, smallest, secret-seeming one
one remembers, severed, lowered into a porcelain vase
and seen so specially while lowering, identical in water-burial
to the violet violets that looked so different from it,
or it may be the darkest yet May-violet, unpicked,
unseen, and still thought of that leads the mind to more,
and more opposed. There grows no gentian,
no gentian-thought more wild, more violet than that here.

NOTES BY SECTION

4. Melk Benedectine Abbey, Melk, Austria. Sanssouci is Frederick the Great's yellow palace in Potsdam, Germany.

8. From *Reminiscences of the Family of Moody Chase, of Shirley, Mass.*, by William Moody Chase, my relative.

9. "If the brightness is a truce" is from Montale's *Motets*, translated by Wm. Arrowsmith.

10. The first line, and the first half of the second are from Carter Smith's poem, "Therefore You Are That Other One You Love."

17. "I received him in the dark. I had come to bear everything bar being seen." Beckett, *Fizzle 2*

21. From *Reminiscences of the Family of Moody Chase, of Shirley, Mass.*, by William Moody Chase, my relative.

22. "The lovely gaze where every eye doth dwell." Shakespeare, Sonnet 5.

23. The bracketed section is from *Gilgamesh*, as translated by David Ferry.

24–27. The first sections are from *Gilgamesh*, as translated by David Ferry. The second sections are from the 1680 will of Anthony Morse of Newbury, Mass. His brother William was a key figure in the only recorded case of supposed witchcraft in Newbury that was ever subjected to a full legal investigation.

30. From a website on the Dresden Green Diamond: <http://famousdiamonds.tripod.com/ dresdengreendiamond.html>.

34. The bracketed section is spoken by Anna Kurz, from an interview quoted by Frederick Taylor in *Dresden: Tuesday, February 13, 1945* by Frederick Taylor. HarperCollins, New York, p. 265.

36. Lines 1-5 are catalog notes from *Renaissance and Baroque Treasury Art. The Green Vault in Dresden*, translated by Daniel Kletke.

40. From *Renaissance and Baroque Treasury Art. The Green Vault in Dresden*, translated by Daniel Kletke.

42. Spoken by Curt Sonntag, air raid warden for the Sarrasani Circus, as recorded by Ernst Gunther, *Sarrasai, Wie er wirklich war* (Berlin, 1991). Quoted in *Dresden: Tuesday, February 13, 1945* by Frederick Taylor. HarperCollins, New York, pp 310, 311.

43. Spoken by the (unnamed) widow of the Chinese acrobat with the Sarrasani Circus, in an interview included in the German documentary series *Der Fahrhundertkreig*, episode on the bomber war against Germany. Quoted in *Dresden: Tuesday, February 13, 1945,* by Frederick Taylor. HarperCollins, New York, pp 311, 312.

53. David Young's translation of a portion of Montale's "Winter Light."

54. Jonathan Galassi's translation of the same.

58, 59, 68, 70. Each begins with catalog notes from *Renaissance and Baroque Treasury Art. The Green Vault in Dresden*, translated by Daniel Kletke.

71. Borges, "The Writing of the God," *Collected Fictions* p 252.

75. Begins with catalog notes from *Renaissance and Baroque Treasury Art. The Green Vault in Dresden,* translated by Daniel Kletke.

79. Excerpted from Pliny, *Natural History II,* Books III–VII. Book IV. xii.

82. wicker: akin to Old Norse "vikja" "to move, turn"

82, 83. These sections correspond, in part, to David Justin's staging for "La Maja Dolorosa," as performed by the American Repertory Ensemble in Austin, Texas, in 2007.

ACKNOWLEDGMENTS

Sections of *Vault* have appeared in *Poetry International, Newfound, The Laurel Review,* Oneiros Broadsides, *Cutbank,* and *Literati Quarterly.* I'm especially grateful for support from The John Simon Guggenheim Foundation, The National Endowment for the Arts, and the Whiting Foundation.

KATHLEEN PEIRCE grew up in Rock Island, Illinois. She received an MFA from The University of Iowa Writers' Workshop, and currently teaches in the MFA program at Texas State University. Her previous books are *Mercy, Divided Touch/Divided Color, The Oval Hour,* and *The Ardors.*

✻

COLOPHON

Text is set in a digital version of Jenson, designed by Robert Slimbach in 1996, and based on the work of punchcutter, printer, and publisher Nicolas Jenson. The titles here are in Futura.

✻

NEW MICHIGAN PRESS, based in Tucson, Arizona, prints poetry and prose chapbooks, especially work that transcends traditional genre. Together with DIAGRAM, NMP sponsors a yearly chapbook competition.

DIAGRAM, a journal of text, art, and schematic, is published bimonthly at THEDIAGRAM.COM. Periodic print anthologies are available from the New Michigan Press at NEWMICHIGANPRESS.COM.

CPSIA information can be obtained
at www.ICGtesting.com
Printed in the USA
LVHW011240140119
603814LV00001B/249/P